IT'S TIME TO LEARN ABOUT COCKROACHES

It's Time to Learn about Cockroaches

Walter the Educator

Silent King Books
A WhichHead Entertainment Imprint

Copyright © 2025 by Walter the Educator

All rights reserved. No part of this book may be reproduced in any manner whatsoever without written per- mission except in the case of brief quotations embodied in critical articles and reviews.

First Printing, 2024

Disclaimer

This book is a literary work; the story is not about specific persons, locations, situations, and/or circumstances unless mentioned in a historical context. Any resemblance to real persons, locations, situations, and/or circumstances is coincidental. This book is for entertainment and informational purposes only. The author and publisher offer this information without warranties expressed or implied. No matter the grounds, neither the author nor the publisher will be accountable for any losses, injuries, or other damages caused by the reader's use of this book. The use of this book acknowledges an understanding and acceptance of this disclaimer.

It's Time to Learn about Cockroaches is a collectible early learning book by Walter the Educator suitable for all ages belonging to Walter the Educator's Time to Eat Book Series. Collect more books at WaltertheEducator.com

USE THE EXTRA SPACE TO TAKE NOTES AND DOCUMENT YOUR MEMORIES

COCKROACHES

In corners dark and places small,

It's Time to Learn about Cockroaches

Cockroaches creep along the wall.

With wiggly legs and busy feet,

They scurry fast and can't be beat!

Their shiny shells are tough and brown,

They love to scamper up and down.

Their long antennae wave and sway,

To help them find their food each day.

Cockroaches hide when lights turn on,

They like the dark where they belong.

Under the sink or near the floor,

They dash and dart and look for more!

They're not so picky when they eat,

Old crumbs and scraps are such a treat.

A cookie crumb, a piece of bread,

Will keep a cockroach happy-fed!

It's Time to Learn about
Cockroaches

They've been around since dinosaurs,

Through ancient times and meteor showers!

Cockroaches lived through heat and snow,

They're tough and smart, they surely know!

Some cockroaches can even fly,

They spread their wings and zoom up high!

But most just run with speedy toes,

To find a place that's safe and close.

They clean up messes on the ground,

Eating things that rot around.

They help the earth by breaking waste,

They work so fast, they move with haste!

If you spot one, don't you scream,

Just stay calm, no need to dream.

It's Time to Learn about
Cockroaches

Cockroaches want to run and hide,

They're more afraid than brave inside.

They love to live where food is near,

So keeping clean keeps them clear.

Sweep the crumbs and shut the door,

And cockroaches will come no more!

So now you know, they're not all bad,

They're part of nature, be glad, not mad!

Little roaches do their part,

It's Time to Learn about
Cockroaches

Helping Earth with all their heart!

ABOUT THE CREATOR

Walter the Educator is one of the pseudonyms for Walter Anderson. Formally educated in Chemistry, Business, and Education, he is an educator, an author, a diverse entrepreneur, and he is the son of a disabled war veteran. "Walter the Educator" shares his time between educating and creating. He holds interests and owns several creative projects that entertain, enlighten, enhance, and educate, hoping to inspire and motivate you. Follow, find new works, and stay up to date with Walter the Educator™

at WaltertheEducator.com

www.ingramcontent.com/pod-product-compliance
Lightning Source LLC
LaVergne TN
LVHW051920060526
838201LV00060B/4093